Mushroom

> Autorin: **Cornelia Schinharl**

Contents

Fundamentals

The Recipes

Appendix

The Flavor Givers

In late summer, as nature slowly adjusts to the coming of fall, the woods are filled with a heavenly scent. If you're lucky, this is the time when you'll find porcini and chanterelle mushrooms. Otherwise, around now you also can still find them for sale at the markets. The rest of the year, you can buy top-quality white, oyster, king oyster, and other fine mushrooms produced by commercial mushroom growers. The different mushroom varieties are usually interchangeable in these recipes. If you do find mushrooms growing wild and are certain that they're edible, you can also use them in place of the commercially cultivated ones.

Basics

> **2** *You can also store mushrooms in a paper bag.*

1 | Buying mushrooms

Fresh mushrooms look plump and dry without being dried out. Brown spots on white or king oyster mushrooms, and dried edges or a slimy appearance on any mushroom means that the mushrooms are too old or have been stored incorrectly. You're better off leaving them alone and finding yourself a new vegetable market. A fresh scent is also an unmistakable indication of quality. Old mushrooms, especially oyster mushrooms, have an almost fishy smell.

2 | Picking mushrooms

Anyone who knows mushrooms well enough to identify them in the woods will be out hunting them in the fall. However, never pick a mushroom unless you are absolutely certain that you know what it is. Experimenting with wild mushrooms can be deadly! So never take a chance. Since it isn't always easy for inexperienced mushroom hunters to distinguish edible mushrooms from edible ones, we did not include wild mushrooms in this book. To hunt mushrooms, you need a good mushroom identification guide that provides detailed descriptions of all the mushrooms' characteristics. That's beyond the scope of a cookbook, but if you're absolutely sure that you have picked edible mushrooms and/or have taken them to a mushroom consultation center for an expert opinion, you'll find many recipes in this book that can also be prepared with wild mushrooms. In any case, we've suggested more than one variety in most recipes.

3 | Storing mushrooms

When you get them home, take the mushrooms out of the package, especially if they're wrapped in plastic, because this causes the mushrooms to "sweat." We recommend that you transfer them to a bowl and keep them in the refrigerator, either in the vegetable bin or directly above it. But don't store them for more than a couple days, because this dries them out and they lose their flavor.

➤ **Important:** Because the protein composition of cooked mushrooms changes quickly, they spoil quickly. This is why you shouldn't keep leftover mushroom dishes for more than one day.

> **1** *Fresh mushrooms are plump and dry, without looking dried out.*

Cleaning and preparing mushrooms

Mushrooms are fairly uncomplicated. They're usually clean when you buy them (especially cultivated mushrooms) and only have to be wiped off with a paper towel. You should never wash them, because they tend to soak up water (especially if you leave them in the water) and lose their flavor. Mushrooms can be cooked in every imaginable way, and require very short cooking times. If you sauté them in a pan, always start at high heat. If this produces liquid, keep stirring until it all evaporates so the dish won't taste watery.

Don't prepare more mushrooms than you can eat. Let leftovers cool immediately and don't store them for more than one day. Cooked mushrooms spoil easily and can also cause indigestion.

Cleaning wild mushrooms

Cut mushroom stems at ground level and immediately use the knife to scrape off all dirt and pine needles. Cut off imperfections and transport mushrooms in a roomy basket without piling them up.

Cleaning cultivated mushrooms

Most cultivated mushrooms are grown on straw, so they aren't dirty. Mushrooms grown in earth may sometimes have dirt on them. Brush them off with a mushroom brush or wipe them off with a paper towel.

Soaking mushrooms

The fastest way to soften dried mushrooms is to soak them in lukewarm water. It can take from 20 minutes to 1 hour, depending on the variety. Afterwards, rinse sandy mushrooms and filter the soaking water.

Cut off the stems?

In the case of porcini, white, cremini, king oyster, chanterelle, and morel mushrooms, you should only trim the very end of the stems. Shiitake, oyster, and cloud ear mushrooms have tough stems that should be removed completely.

Store-bought mushrooms

White and cremini mushrooms:
These mushrooms come from France, where they're known as "champignons." Although they also grow in fields and meadows, people generally use the commercially cultivated type. Cremini are brown mushrooms that are usually more intensely flavorful. They're also available in a larger form, called portobello.
Preparation: Both taste great cooked or raw.

Oyster mushrooms:
Originally from Southeast Asia, where they grow in forests on rotten tree stumps. They've become increasingly popular as cultivated mushrooms, in which case they're grown on straw, meaning they're free of earth or other dirt. Oyster mushrooms have a delicate and aromatic flavor and remain tender when sautéed.
Preparation: Oyster mushrooms are not very good raw. When cooked, they're best sautéed or grilled.

Shiitake mushrooms:
Shiitakes originated in China, where they have been cultivated on wooden logs for centuries. In this country they're usually grown on compressed sawdust. Shiitakes are available fresh or dried and have an intense flavor. If dried, they have to be soaked in warm water for about 30 minutes. They can be found in Asian markets and larger supermarkets.
Preparation: Shiitakes go best in Asian dishes, although they can also give other mushroom dishes an intense flavor.

Morels:
These long, thin mushrooms with a honeycomb structure are expensive and not always available. You'll find them dried in gourmet shops and in the food section of larger supermarkets. They have such an intense aroma that you don't need very many. From April to June, you can sometimes find them fresh in markets.
Preparation: Since the morel's "honeycombs" may contain sand, always rinse them well. Then sauté or braise.

Chanterelle mushrooms:

Chanterelles grow in deciduous and coniferous forests and can be purchased at any market in the late summer and fall. These reddish-yellow mushrooms taste best when small. Because dirt can lodge between the gills, you need to inspect them carefully and clean them as necessary. It's best to use a small bristle brush.

Preparation: Chanterelles taste great sautéed, but are also very good braised and in cream sauces.

Porcini mushrooms:

Porcini mushrooms grow in coniferous and beech forests and are definitely our favorite edible mushrooms. In late summer you can purchase them fresh. At all other times, they're available dried, in which case their fragrance and flavor are even more intense. You can even eat the stems and the tubes under the caps. You only need to remove the tubes on large mushrooms where the network is especially thick.

Preparation: Porcini mushrooms are delicious raw as carpaccio and cooked in any form.

King oyster mushrooms:

A new variety, at least in a cultivated form, king oyster mushrooms are primarily available in health food stores. These mushrooms have firm and very tasty flesh. Their beige-to-dark-brown caps stay relatively small. Only the tips of the stems need to be removed; all the rest is edible.

Preparation: King oyster mushrooms are especially delicious sautéed, grilled, or braised.

Cloud ear mushrooms:

These Chinese dried tree mushrooms are also called mo-er mushrooms. You'll find them in any supermarket. Before using, soak them in warm water for about 20 minutes and they will expand to about five times their size. Usually, part of the stem remains hard, so trim off a generous amount.

Preparation: Cloud ear mushrooms taste best in Asian dishes, cooked either in a wok or in a pot of soup.

7

Preserving mushrooms

Mushrooms in oil:

Clean 2¼ pounds small mushrooms (e.g. chanterelles or cremini) and boil in a mixture of 2 cups white wine vinegar, 1 cup white wine, and salt for 10 minutes. Dry thoroughly with a kitchen towel. Place in two half-size jars with some organic lemon peel, 2 bay leaves, and 2 sprigs rosemary. Add enough olive oil to cover mushrooms completely. Seal tightly. Will keep for about three months. Wait at least one week before opening.

Mushrooms in vinegar:

Clean 2¼ pounds white or cremini mushrooms and brown in 4 tablespoons olive oil. Add 1 tablespoon capers, 4 peeled garlic cloves, 2 dried chile peppers, the leaves from 1 bunch basil, ⅓ cup balsamic or other spiced vinegar and 1⅔ cups water. Season with salt and boil for about 3 minutes. Pour mushrooms and hot liquid into two sealed jars and clasp tightly. Will keep for about one month and taste best after about one week.

Drying mushrooms:

If you find a lot of porcini (or other mushrooms) in the woods, you can dry some of them and thereby render them even tastier. Clean mushrooms and slice thinly. Place on a baking sheet lined with parchment paper as close together as possible and heat in a 150°F oven (wedge oven door open with a wooden spoon), turning occasionally, until they're thoroughly dried. If the weather is hot, you can also dry them in the sun.

Freezing mushrooms:

You can also preserve large quantities of mushrooms by freezing them. Clean the mushrooms, slice, spread out side-by-side on a tray and pre-freeze for about 1 hour. Then transfer to freezer bags, seal, and freeze. Pre-freezing makes it easier to separate the frozen mushrooms later on. Freezing doesn't have much effect on the flavor of the mushrooms, but after thawing they'll be too moist to sauté. Roast or braise them instead.

Fancy mushrooms: truffles

Truffles grow underground on the roots of deciduous trees, such as oak and beech. They're tuberous like potatoes and can be walnut- to fist-sized. They also have a very strong odor, which must be why they're hunted by specially trained dogs or even pigs. Most truffles in Europe come from Italy or France. Because they're rare, these coveted, fancy mushrooms are rather expensive.

Although there are many varieties, the most well-known are black truffles, which are considered the fanciest and usually come from France; white truffles, which grow in Piedmont, especially around the city of Alba; and summer truffles, which look like black truffles on the outside, but have light interiors. Besides fresh truffles, you can also purchase preserved truffles. It's best to store fresh truffles in a screw-top jar.

Cleaning truffles

Never rinse these knobby mushrooms. Instead, brush off the dirt with a hard-bristle brush. Then slice very thinly with a sharp knife.

Slicing truffles

In order for them to yield their full aroma, truffles are sliced. The best tool is a special truffle slicer. You can adjust the opening to shave off slices ranging from thick to paper-thin.

Carpaccio with truffles

Freeze beef tenderloin only slightly and cut into paper-thin slices. Arrange on plates and drizzle with lemon juice and olive oil. Season lightly with salt and pepper and shave white truffles over the top.

Pasta with truffles

Cook ribbon noodles (preferably fresh) in salted water until al dente and drain. Toss in melted butter, mixing in a little grated Parmesan. Season with salt and pepper, transfer to plates, and shave (black or white) truffles over the top.

Appetizers, Salads, and Snacks

Is it hard for you to imagine enjoying a leisurely meal without starting it off with an appetizer—say, crusty bread slices with spiced mushrooms or a fresh salad? Here you'll find a number of delightful mushroom recipes that will give your meal a proper start.

Quick Recipes

Mushroom Bruschetta

SERVES 4

➤ ¾ lb porcini or cremini mushrooms |
2 cloves garlic | 3 tbs olive oil | Salt |
Freshly ground pepper | ½ bunch basil |
8 toasted bread slices

1 | Clean mushrooms, peel garlic, and slice both finely.

2 | In a pan, heat 2 tablespoons olive oil and sauté mushrooms over medium heat for about 5 minutes while stirring. Season with salt and pepper.

3 | Cut basil leaves into thin strips and toss basil and remaining 1 tablespoon olive oil with mushrooms. Arrange on bread slices.

Chile Mushrooms

SERVES 4:

➤ 2 red chile peppers | ½ bunch parsley |
¾ lb white or cremini mushrooms |
4 tbs olive oil | 2 tsp honey |
2 tsp balsamic vinegar | Salt

1 | Rinse chile peppers, remove stems, and cut into fine rings with seeds. Rinse parsley, shake dry, and chop leaves finely. Clean mushrooms and cut into quarters.

2 | In a pan, heat olive oil and sauté mushrooms and chiles over medium heat for about 5 minutes while stirring. Add honey and sauté a little longer. Season to taste with vinegar and salt and stir in parsley. Delicious with toast or a salad.

Asian | Easy

Marinated Mushrooms

SERVES 4:

➤ 1 lb white or shiitake mushrooms

1 organic lime

1 piece fresh ginger (about 1 inch)

1 red chile pepper

4 cloves garlic

3 tbs oil

2 tbs soy sauce

Salt

1 handful cilantro leaves

🕐 Prep time: 25 minutes
🕐 Marinating time: 4 hours
➤ Calories/serving: About 90

1 | Clean mushrooms. Cut white mushrooms into quarters. Remove stems from shiitakes and cut large mushrooms in half. Rinse lime under hot water, cut off a thin layer of peel, and cut into strips. Squeeze out juice.

2 | Peel ginger and chop finely. Rinse chile pepper, remove stem, and cut into fine rings with seeds. Peel garlic and cut into very thin slices.

3 | In a saucepan, heat oil and sauté mushrooms over medium heat for 2–3 minutes while stirring. Add ginger, garlic and chile pepper, and sauté briefly. Pour in soy sauce, 2 tablespoons lime juice and ¼ cup water, simmer for 5 minutes, and season with salt.

4 | Marinate mushrooms at room temperature for 4 hours. Add seasoning to taste and sprinkle with cilantro leaves and lime peel.

➤ Side dishes: Chapatis, tortillas

➤ Beverages: Cold beer, dry sherry

For Company | Fast

Mushroom Carpaccio

SERVES 4:

➤ ¼ tsp mustard (Dijon or honey mustard)

2 tbs lemon juice

6 tbs cold-pressed olive oil

Salt

Freshly ground pepper

⅔ lb very fresh white or cremini mushrooms

1 thin celery stalk

2 green onions

½ bunch basil

🕐 Prep time: 25 minutes
Calories/serving: About 150

1 | Mix mustard, lemon juice, oil, salt, and pepper to form a creamy sauce.

2 | Clean mushrooms, slice as thinly as possible, and spread out on 4 plates. Pour sauce evenly over the top. Let stand for about 15 minutes.

3 | In the meantime, rinse celery, clean, and dice very finely. Rinse green onions, clean, and chop into fine rings, including the green parts. Shred basil leaves. Combine celery, onion rings and basil, and sprinkle over the mushrooms.

➤ Side dish: White bread
➤ Beverage: White wine

TIP

Instead of celery, use 1 tomato or 1 small bell pepper.

If desired, you can also shave a little Parmesan over the carpaccio.

Photo top: **Marinated Mushrooms**   *Photo bottom:* **Mushroom Carpaccio** ➤

Also Delicious Cold

Stuffed Mushrooms

SERVES 4:

- ➤ ⅔ lb large cremini or white mushrooms
  Salt
  Freshly ground pepper
  4 tbs dry white wine (optional)
  1 medium tomato
  ⅓ lb raw bratwurst (about 5 oz)
  ½ ball mozzarella (about 2 oz)
  2 sprigs thyme
  2 cloves garlic
  2 tbs olive oil

🕐 Prep time: 35 minutes
➤ Calories/serving: About 210

1 | Preheat oven to 450°F. Clean mushrooms and twist off stems. In a small bowl, dice stems finely and mix with salt, pepper, and wine in a baking dish.

2 | Rinse tomatoes, remove cores, and dice very finely. Squeeze bratwurst out of the skin. Dice mozzarella. Rinse thyme, shake dry, and strip off leaves. Peel garlic and squeeze through a press.

3 | Knead together tomato, mozzarella, sausage, thyme, garlic, salt, and pepper and use to fill mushroom caps.

4 | Place mushrooms in the baking dish, drizzle with olive oil, and bake in the oven (middle rack) for 18–20 minutes.

- ➤ Side dishes: Arugula or mâche salad and white bread
- ➤ Beverage: White wine

Can Prepare in Advance

Mushrooms Topped with Breadcrumbs

SERVES 4:

- ➤ ⅔ lb oyster or porcini mushrooms
  8 tbs olive oil
  1 organic lemon
  1 large bunch fresh parsley
  1 green onion
  2 cloves garlic
  ¼ cup breadcrumbs
  2 tbs freshly grated Parmesan
  Salt
  Freshly ground pepper

🕐 Prep time: 30 minutes
➤ Calories/serving: About 275

1 | Preheat oven to 450°F. Clean mushrooms and remove stems. Leave oyster mushrooms whole or cut porcini caps lengthwise into 2–3 pieces. Brush mushrooms with oil and arrange side-by-side in a baking dish.

2 | Rinse lemon in hot water and remove a thin layer of peel. Rinse parsley, shake dry, and pluck off leaves. Rinse green onion, clean, and chop coarsely. Peel garlic. Combine garlic, lemon peel, parsley, and green onion and chop as finely as possible.

3 | Combine parsley mixture, breadcrumbs, Parmesan, and remaining oil and season with salt and pepper. Distribute on mushrooms and bake in the oven (middle rack) for 12–15 minutes until golden-brown. Let cool and serve.

- ➤ Side dishes: Crusty white bread and lemon wedges
- ➤ Beverages: Dry white wine, prosecco

Easy | Fast

Grilled Mushrooms

SERVES 4:

- ➤ ⅔ lb large cremini, oyster, or porcini mushrooms
- ½ organic lemon
- 4 cloves garlic
- ½ bunch fresh parsley (optional)
- 1 small piece red chile pepper
- 6 tbs olive oil
- Salt
- Freshly ground pepper

🕒 Prep time: 30 minutes
🕒 Marinating time: 1–4 hours
➤ Calories/serving: About 160

1 | Clean mushrooms. Remove stems from oyster mushrooms. Leave oyster mushrooms whole, otherwise cut in half lengthwise.

2 | Rinse lemon half under hot water, grate off zest, and squeeze out juice. Peel garlic and slice finely. Rinse parsley, shake dry, and chop leaves finely. Rinse chile piece and chop very finely.

3 | Combine lemon peel, lemon juice, garlic, parsley, chile, and olive oil and distribute on mushrooms. Marinate for 1–4 hours.

4 | Heat oven broiler or charcoal grill. Scrape off marinade, season mushrooms with salt and pepper, and grill over the coals or under the broiler for 3–4 minutes. Brush with marinade, turn, and grill for another 3–4 minutes.

➤ Side dishes: White bread, lamb chops

Also Delicious Cold

Mushroom Frittata

SERVES 4:

- ➤ ¾ lb assorted mushrooms
- 1 onion
- 2 cloves garlic
- ½ bunch fresh oregano
- 1 tbs chopped walnuts (may substitute pine nuts)
- 4 tbs olive oil
- 1 tbs lemon juice
- 8 eggs
- Salt
- Freshly ground pepper
- 1 tsp Hungarian hot paprika
- 2 tbs freshly grated Parmesan

🕒 Prep time: 40 minutes
➤ Calories/serving: About 305

1 | Clean mushrooms and dice finely. Peel onion and garlic and chop finely. Rinse oregano, shake dry, and chop leaves finely.

2 | Place walnuts in an ungreased pan, toast briefly, and remove. Heat 2 tablespoons olive oil in the pan and sauté mushrooms, onion, and garlic over high heat for about 5 minutes. Stir in oregano and lemon juice.

3 | Whisk eggs lightly and season with salt, pepper, and paprika. Stir in mushrooms, walnuts, and Parmesan.

4 | Add remaining oil to the pan and heat. Pour in egg-mushroom mixture and cook over low heat for 15–20 minutes until it becomes firm. Turn carefully and fry for another 5 minutes. Serve lukewarm or cooled.

➤ Side dish: Tomato salad

For Company | Easy
Arugula Salad with Fried Mushrooms

SERVES 4:

- 2 bunches arugula
  1 small head radicchio
  ¾ lb king oyster, porcini, or oyster mushrooms
  1 tsp honey
  2 tbs balsamic vinegar
  7 tbs olive oil
  Salt
  Freshly ground pepper
  2 tbs pine nuts

🕐 Prep time: 30 minutes
➤ Calories/serving: About 245

1 | Sort arugula and trim thick stems. Separate radicchio leaves and tear into bite-sized pieces. Rinse radicchio and arugula and spin thoroughly dry.

2 | Clean mushrooms and cut into thin slices or strips about ⅛ inch thick. For the sauce, combine honey, vinegar, and 4 tablespoons olive oil. Mix sauce well and season with salt and pepper.

3 | Heat an ungreased pan and toast pine nuts while stirring until golden. Remove from pan. Add remaining oil to the pan, add mushrooms, and stir. Sauté over medium heat for 6-8 minutes while stirring. Season to taste with salt and pepper. Distribute salad and pine nuts on plates and drizzle with sauce. Top with hot mushrooms and serve immediately.

➤ Side dish: Olive ciabatta

Fast | Inexpensive
Mâche Salad with Bacon Mushrooms

SERVES 4:

- ¾ cup mâche (about 7 oz)
  ½ cup sliced bacon
  ½ lb cremini or white mushrooms
  3 tbs apple juice (preferably unfiltered)
  1 tsp hot mustard
  1 tbs balsamic vinegar
  2 tbs olive oil
  Freshly ground pepper
  Salt (optional)

🕐 Prep time: 20 minutes
➤ Calories/serving: About 260

1 | Rinse mâche thoroughly and spin dry. Distribute on 4 plates.

2 | Cut bacon into fine strips and render in a pan over medium heat for about 5 minutes until nice and crispy.

3 | In the meantime, clean mushrooms and cut into quarters. Add to bacon and fry for 5 minutes. Combine apple juice, mustard, vinegar, and olive oil and season with pepper. Add mixture to mushrooms and salt lightly if desired. Distribute evenly over the mâche.

➤ Side dish: Whole-wheat baguette
➤ Beverage: Light red wine

TIP

If desired, you can also sprinkle some diced tomato over the finished arugula salad.

For Company | Fruity

Mushroom Salad with Grapes

SERVES 4:

➤ 2 bunches green onions
²⁄₃ lb cremini, white, or chanterelle mushrooms
1¹⁄₃ cups blue grapes
1 tbs chopped walnuts
¹⁄₂ cup dry white wine (may substitute vegetable stock)
1 tsp hot mustard
2 tsp honey
2 tbs white balsamic vinegar
4 tbs olive oil
Salt
Freshly ground pepper
1 handful fresh chervil

🕐 Prep time: 25 minutes
➤ Calories/serving: About 200

1 | Rinse and clean green onions and cut into strips about 2 inches long. Clean mushrooms and cut in half. Rinse grapes, cut in half and, if necessary, remove seeds. Break walnuts into small pieces.

2 | Combine wine, mustard, honey, and vinegar.

3 | In a pan, heat oil and sauté mushrooms and onions over medium heat for 5 minutes, heat while stirring. Stir in grapes and walnuts, season with salt and pepper, and transfer to 4 plates.

4 | Pour wine mixture into the pan and bring to a boil over high heat. Season to taste with salt and pepper and drizzle over the salad ingredients. Rinse chervil, spin dry, and sprinkle leaves over the salad.

➤ Side dish: Baguette
➤ Beverage: White wine

Mediterranean

Bell Pepper Salad with Mushrooms

SERVES 4:

➤ 2 red bell peppers
2 zucchini (about ³⁄₄ lb)
5 tbs olive oil
1 tbs lemon juice
Salt
Freshly ground pepper
²⁄₃ lb oyster, porcini, or portobello mushrooms

2 cloves garlic
¹⁄₂ bunch fresh basil
1 tbs balsamic vinegar

🕐 Prep time: 45 minutes
➤ Calories/serving: About 170

1 | Preheat oven to 475°F. Rinse bell peppers, cut in half, and clean. Place on a baking sheet with the cut sides down and bake in the oven for 15 minutes.

2 | Rinse zucchini, clean, and cut into sticks ¹⁄₄ inch across. In a baking dish, mix 3 tablespoons oil, lemon juice, salt, and pepper. Clean mushrooms and cut up larger ones. Mix with zucchini.

3 | Cover bell peppers with a damp cloth. Roast zucchini and mushrooms in the oven (middle rack) for about 10 minutes, turning once.

4 | Peel bell peppers and cut into strips. Peel garlic and slice finely. Cut basil into strips.

5 | Toss vegetables, garlic and basil with remaining oil and vinegar, season with salt and pepper, and serve lukewarm.

Fruity | For Company
Cream of Morel Soup with Pears

SERVES 4:

➤ 2 tsp dried morels
2 shallots
3 tbs butter
1 tbs flour
1 jar vegetable stock (about 1¾ cups)
1 firm pear (about ½ lb)
1 tbs sugar
Salt
Freshly ground pepper
1 tsp lemon juice
¼ cup crème fraîche

🕐 Prep time: 20 minutes
🕐 Soaking time: 1 hour
➤ Calories/serving: About 180

1 | Soak morels in ¼ cup lukewarm water for 1 hour to soften. Then transfer to a colander, rinse thoroughly, and cut into strips. Filter water used for soaking and reserve.

2 | Peel shallots, dice finely, and braise half in butter over medium heat. Braise morels briefly. Dust with flour and sauté briefly. Add stock, reserved soaking water, and ¾ cup water. Simmer soup uncovered for about 10 minutes.

3 | In the meantime, cut pear into quarters, remove core, peel, and cut into wedges. Melt remaining butter with sugar over medium heat. Sauté pear wedges for 3–4 minutes until nicely browned. Season lightly with salt and pepper and add lemon juice.

4 | Refine soup with crème fraîche and season with salt and pepper. Garnish with pears and serve in preheated soup plates.

Spicy | Easy
Asian Soup with Shiitake Mushrooms

SERVES 4:

➤ ⅓ lb shiitake mushrooms
½ lb green asparagus
1 piece fresh ginger (about 1 inch)
1 stalk lemon grass
1 red chile pepper
1 jar Asian stock (about 1¾ cups; may substitute chicken stock)
2 tbs soy sauce
2 green onions
4 sprigs fresh cilantro
4 tsp sesame oil

🕐 Prep time: 20 minutes
➤ Calories/serving: About 245

1 | Clean shiitakes, remove stems, and slice thinly. Rinse asparagus, peel bottom third, cut off ends, and cut into ¼ inch pieces.

2 | Peel ginger and cut into fine matchsticks. Rinse lemon grass and cut into pieces 1 inch long. Rinse chile pepper, clean, and cut into rings.

3 | Combine stock, 1¾ cups water, lemon grass, ginger, chile pepper, and soy sauce and bring to a boil. Add mushrooms and asparagus and simmer over medium heat for about 5 minutes until al dente.

4 | Rinse green onions, clean, and cut into fine rings. Rinse cilantro, shake dry, and pluck off leaves. Transfer soup to 4 bowls, drizzle with oil, and garnish with onion rings and cilantro.

Mushrooms with Pasta, Rice, etc.

Do you like pasta, rice, and polenta? Do you love to eat mushrooms? Then you've struck gold, because mushrooms are the perfect accompaniment to the other three. Whether in a creamy sauce, with vegetables, or with cheese, whether European or Asian, all the recipes in this chapter are easy to make and simply delicious!

Quick Recipes

Glass Noodles and Mushrooms

SERVES 4:

➤ ½ lb glass noodles │ 1 lb oyster mushrooms │ 1 leek │ 2 cloves garlic │ 4 tbs oil │ ⅓ cup vegetable stock │ 4 tbs fish sauce │ 4 tbs lime juice │ Salt

1 │ Soak glass noodles in warm water for 10 minutes, then drain, and cut up with kitchen scissors.

2 │ Clean mushrooms and cut into strips. Clean leak, slit open lengthwise, rinse, and cut into strips. Peel garlic and slice.

3 │ Sauté mushrooms, leek, and garlic in oil over high heat for 5 minutes. Add stock, stir in noodles, and heat. Season with fish sauce, lime juice, and salt.

Spaghetti with Mushrooms

SERVES 4:

➤ ¾ lb porcini or cremini mushrooms │ ¾ lb spaghetti │ Salt │ ½ bunch fresh parsley │ 2 shallots │ 3 tbs olive oil │ 1 tbs butter │ Freshly ground pepper

1 │ Clean mushrooms and slice finely. Cook pasta in a salted water according to package directions until al dente. Rinse parsley, shake dry, and chop leaves finely. Peel shallots, cut in half, and cut into fine strips.

2 │ Heat oil and butter and sauté mushrooms over high heat for 2 minutes. Add shallots and parsley, cover, and braise over low heat for 6 minutes. Season with salt and pepper. Toss well with drained spaghetti.

25

Zesty | For Company

Pasta with Mushroom Arugula Fish

SERVES 4:

➤ ¾ lb white, cremini, or porcini mushrooms
  1 tbs lemon juice
  1 large bunch fresh arugula
  ⅓ lb salmon fillet (about 5 oz; may substitute salmon trout fillet)
  Salt
  ¾ lb narrow ribbon pasta
  1 tbs olive oil
  1 tbs butter
  ⅔ cup heavy cream
  1 tbs pine nuts
  Freshly ground pepper

🕐 Prep time: 25 minutes
➤ Calories/serving: About 615

1 | Clean mushrooms and slice finely. Mix with lemon juice. Sort arugula and remove tough stems. Then rinse, spin dry, and chop coarsely. Cut fish into strips ½–¾ inch wide.

2 | Bring salted water to a boil. Cook pasta according to package directions until al dente.

3 | In the meantime, heat oil and butter and sauté mushrooms over medium heat for about 3 minutes while stirring. Add arugula and let wilt. Add cream. Stir in fish, cover, and simmer over low heat for 2 minutes.

4 | In an ungreased pan, toast pine nuts until golden. Season pasta sauce with salt and pepper. Drain pasta and transfer to preheated plates. Distribute sauce on top and sprinkle with pine nuts.

➤ Beverage: Dry white wine

Hearty | Fast

Pasta and Saffron Mushrooms

SERVES 4:

➤ ¼ lb raw, smoked ham
  1 bunch green onions
  ⅔ lb porcini, chanterelle, or cremini mushrooms
  ¾ lb wide tube pasta
  Salt
  2 tbs oil
  ½ cup dry white wine (may substitute vegetable stock)
  1 small jar saffron (0.1 g)
  1 pinch ground coriander
  1 tsp lemon juice
  ½ bunch fresh basil

🕐 Prep time: 20 minutes
➤ Calories/serving: About 540

1 | Remove fatty edges from ham and cut into strips. Rinse green onions, clean, cut into pieces 2 inches long, and then cut into strips. Clean mushrooms. Slice porcini or cremini mushrooms.

2 | Cook pasta in salted water according to package directions until al dente. Sauté ham and onions in oil over medium heat for 1–2 minutes. Add mushrooms and sauté for 2 minutes.

3 | Pour wine over mushrooms and season with saffron, coriander, lemon juice, and salt. Chop basil leaves finely. Drain pasta and toss with mushrooms and basil.

➤ Beverage: White wine

Can Prepare in Advance | Inexpensive

Mushroom Spinach Lasagna

SERVES 4:

➤ 2 lb spinach leaves

Salt

1⅓ lb white or cremini mushrooms

2 tbs olive oil

1 organic lemon

4 cloves garlic

2 tbs butter

2 tbs flour

2 cups milk

½ lb Gorgonzola (about 7 oz)

¼ cup freshly grated Parmesan

Freshly ground pepper

½ lb lasagna noodles (do not precook)

🕐 Prep time: 1¼ hours

➤ Calories/serving: About 680

1 | Prepare spinach. Cook in boiling, salted water only until it wilts, rinse under cold water, drain well, and chop coarsely. Clean mushrooms, slice thinly, and sauté in oil over high heat for 3–4 minutes. Season with salt and let cool.

2 | Rinse lemon under hot water, remove a thin layer of peel, and chop finely. Peel garlic and chop finely. Mix mushrooms, spinach, lemon peel, and garlic.

3 | Melt butter and sauté flour until golden while stirring constantly. Beat in milk with a wire whisk and simmer

béchamel sauce over low heat for 5–10 minutes.

4 | Dice Gorgonzola. Stir Gorgonzola and Parmesan into the sauce and season to taste with salt and pepper.

5 | Preheat oven to 375°F. Pour a little sauce into a baking dish. Fill with alternating layers of lasagna noodles, mushrooms, spinach, and sauce, ending with remaining sauce.

6 | Bake lasagna in the oven (middle rack) for about 40 minutes until the noodles are soft and the surface is browned.

1 Prepare mushrooms

Sort spinach leaves to remove any wilted ones, cut off thick stems, and rinse well.

2 Cook béchamel

Sauté flour in butter until golden while stirring constantly. Gradually beat in milk.

3 Arrange in layers

Arrange ingredients in baking dish, alternating layers as follows: Sauce, noodles, vegetables, layer of sauce.

29

Vegetarian | Inexpensive

Mushroom Dumplings with Bell Pepper Ragout

SERVES 4:

- ➤ 1½ lb king oyster mushrooms
- 4 tbs olive oil
- 6 slices stale white bread
- 1 bunch parsley
- 1 onion
- 2 large eggs
- Salt
- Freshly ground pepper
- 2 red bell peppers
- 1 eggplant
- ¾ cup vegetable stock
- 1 tbs small capers (may substitute pitted olives)

🕓 Prep time: 1 hour
➤ Calories/serving: About 345

1 | Clean mushrooms and dice very finely. Sauté in half the oil over high heat for about 5 minutes.

2 | Cut bread into cubes and soak in a little lukewarm water for 10 minutes. Rinse parsley, shake dry, and chop leaves finely. Peel onion and mince. Purée half the mushrooms finely.

3 | Squeeze out bread thoroughly, crush finely, and knead together with mushrooms, parsley, onion, and eggs to form a smooth dough. Season with salt and pepper and shape into 8 equal-sized dumplings.

4 | Rinse bell peppers and eggplant, clean, cut into ¼ inch cubes and brown in remaining oil. Add stock and season with capers, salt, and pepper. Cover and stew over low heat for 10 minutes.

5 | At the same time, cook dumplings in lightly simmering water for 10 minutes until done. Remove and serve with the vegetables.

Easy | Fast

Mushroom Polenta

SERVES 4:

- ➤ 1⅓ lb porcini, cremini, or chanterelle mushrooms
- 1 onion
- 4 sprigs fresh rosemary
- 2 tbs olive oil
- 2 qt vegetable stock (about 8½ cups; may substitute meat stock)
- ¾ cup instant polenta
- Salt
- Freshly ground pepper
- ⅓ lb cherry tomatoes
- ⅓ lb fontina cheese (about 5¼ oz)
- 1 tbs pine nuts

🕓 Prep time: 25 minutes
➤ Calories/serving: About 465

1 | Clean mushrooms; slice porcini or cremini and leave chanterelles whole. Peel onion, cut into quarters, and cut into fine strips. Rinse rosemary, shake dry, strip off needles, and chop.

2 | In a stockpot, heat oil and sauté over high heat for 3–4 minutes. Add rosemary and onion and sauté briefly. Add stock and bring to a boil. Stir in polenta and season with salt and pepper. Cover and cook over low heat for 5 minutes.

3 | Rinse tomatoes and cut in half, cut up cheese finely, and place both on the polenta. Cover and heat for about 3–4 minutes until the cheese has melted. In an ungreased pan, toast pine nuts until golden and sprinkle on top.

Specialty of Italy
Mushroom Risotto

SERVES 4:

➤ 2 tsp dried porcini mushrooms

1 bunch green onions

2 cloves garlic

²/₃ lb white, porcini, or king oyster mushrooms

½ organic lemon

3 tbs butter

1¾ cups risotto rice

4¼ generous cups vegetable stock

1 bunch wild garlic (may substitute fresh basil)

4 tbs freshly grated Parmesan

Salt

Freshly ground pepper

🕐 Prep time: 50 minutes

➤ Calories/serving: About 515

1 | Soak dried mushrooms in 1 cup lukewarm water for 30 minutes and chop finely (save water).

2 | Rinse green onions, clean, and cut into fine rings. Peel garlic and dice finely. Clean fresh mushrooms and dice. Rinse lemon under hot water, remove a thin layer of peel, and cut into strips. Squeeze out juice.

3 | Melt half the butter and braise green onions, garlic, and all the mushrooms. Add rice and the water used to soak mushrooms.

4 | Season rice with lemon peel and cook uncovered over medium heat for 20–30 minutes. Keep adding more stock, stirring frequently.

5 | Rinse wild garlic, spin dry, and cut into fine strips. When the rice is al dente, stir in Parmesan and remaining butter. Season with salt, pepper, and lemon juice.

➤ Goes with: Freshly grated Parmesan

Asian | Fast
Fried Rice

SERVES 4:

➤ 10 dried cloud ear mushrooms

1 red bell pepper

1 leek

²/₃ cup snow peas

⅓ lb oyster or shiitake mushrooms

3 shallots

4 tbs oil

2²/₃ cups cooked long-grain rice

2 tbs soy sauce

Salt

2 eggs

🕐 Prep time: 30 minutes

➤ Calories/serving: About 715

1 | Soak cloud ear mushrooms in lukewarm water for 20 minutes. Clean vegetables and fresh mushrooms, rinsing if necessary. Cut bell pepper, leek, and mushrooms into thin strips. Peel shallots and cut into fine rings.

2 | In a large pan or wok, heat 2 tablespoons oil. Add rice, spread out evenly, and sauté over high heat for 2 minutes without stirring. Then stir and remove from the pan.

3 | In the remaining oil, sauté vegetables, all the mushrooms, and shallots for about 5 minutes until al dente. Add soy sauce, stir in rice, and season with salt. Whisk eggs, stir into rice, and cook just until they set.

Photo top: **Fried Rice**   *Photo bottom:* **Mushroom Risotto** ➤

Mushrooms with Vegetables and Potatoes

Mushrooms go equally well with vegetables and potatoes, with or without meat. Whether you prepare aromatic porcini gnocchi, treat yourself to a hearty mushroom potato pancake, or pamper yourself with mushrooms in a delicately fruity orange sauce, mushrooms keep popping up in new combinations that are all gastronomically appealing. Try them yourself!

Quick Recipes

Mushrooms in Mustard Sauce

SERVES 4:

➤ 1⅓ lb cremini mushrooms | 1 large bunch wild garlic | 3 tbs butter | ⅔ cup vegetable stock | 1 tbs hot mustard | ⅔ cup heavy cream | 3 tsp lemon juice | Salt | Freshly ground pepper

1 | Clean mushrooms and slice finely. Rinse wild garlic, spin dry, and cut into strips.

2 | In a large pan, melt butter and sauté mushrooms over high heat for about 3–4 minutes while stirring. Stir in wild garlic.

3 | Stir in stock, mustard, and cream. Reduce sauce until thick and creamy and season with lemon juice, salt, and pepper. Serve with potato purée.

Pan-Fried Savoy Cabbage Mushrooms

SERVES 4:

➤ 1 lb savoy cabbage | ⅔ lb any type of mushrooms | 1 onion | ¼ lb streaky smoked bacon | 1 tbs oil | ¾ cup meat stock | Salt | 1 tsp ground caraway | ⅔ cup sour cream

1 | Clean savoy cabbage, rinse, and cut into strips ¼ inch wide. Clean mushrooms and cut into thick slices.

2 | Peel onion, chop bacon finely, and sauté in oil over medium heat for 2 minutes. Add mushrooms and sauté for 2 minutes. Add cabbage and sauté for 1 minute.

3 | Pour stock onto vegetables and season with salt and caraway. Cover and cook for 10 minutes. Stir in sour cream.

Fast | Easy
Multicolor Pan-Fried Mushrooms

SERVE 4:

➤ 1½ lb mixed mushrooms (preferably porcini, chanterelle, and small white mushrooms)
½ lb cherry tomatoes
½ bunch fresh thyme
2 cloves garlic
3 tbs olive oil
Salt
Freshly ground pepper
Cayenne pepper
1 pinch sugar

⏱ Prep time: 20 minutes
➤ Calories/serving: About 110

1 | Clean mushrooms. Cut porcini mushrooms into thin slices and leave chanterelles and white mushrooms whole or cut in half. Rinse tomatoes and cut in half.

2 | Rinse thyme, shake dry, and strip off leaves. Peel garlic and cut into thin slices.

3 | In a large pan, heat oil and stir-fry mushrooms over high heat for 5 minutes. Add thyme and garlic and fry briefly.

4 | Stir in tomatoes. Season to taste with salt, pepper, cayenne, and sugar and let stand for another 1–2 minutes.

➤ Side dish: Fried potatoes, pasta, or white bread
➤ Beverage: Light red wine

Inexpensive | Vegetarian
Breaded Mushrooms

SERVES 4:

➤ 1¾ lb firm potatoes
Salt
1 cup hearty vegetable stock
½ tbs hot mustard
3 tbs white wine vinegar
Freshly ground pepper
8 tbs oil
1⅓ lb large mushrooms (e.g. oyster, portobello, or porcini mushrooms)
¼ cup flour
½ cup breadcrumbs
2 eggs
1 small cucumber

⏱ Prep time: 45 minutes
➤ Calories/serving: About 520

1 | Cook potatoes in salted water for about 20 minutes until tender, but not too tender.

2 | Heat stock and stir in mustard, vinegar, salt, pepper, and 3 tablespoons oil. Let potatoes cool just enough to handle, peel, and slice thinly. Mix with the sauce and let stand until the mushrooms are done.

3 | Clean mushrooms and cut larger ones in half lengthwise. Spread flour and breadcrumbs on separate plates. Whisk eggs on another plate. Moisten mushrooms slightly with water, dredge in flour, dip in eggs, and dredge in breadcrumbs.

4 | Heat remaining oil and fry mushrooms over medium heat for 3–4 minutes on each side. In the meantime, peel cucumber, slice thinly, and mix with potato salad. Add seasoning to taste and serve with mushrooms.

➤ Side dish: Lemon wedges
➤ Beverage: Weiss or pale beer

Easy | For Company
Mushroom Potato Fritters

SERVE 4:

➤ 1 tbs dried
  porcini mushrooms
  1 ½ lb floury potatoes
  ¾ lb white or cremini
  mushrooms
  2 green onions
  Several stalks fresh
  chervil (may substitute
  fresh parsley)
  1 egg
  4 tbs flour
  Salt
  Freshly ground pepper
  1½ tbs butter
  1½ tbs oil

🕐 Prep time: 45 minutes
➤ Calories/serving: About 240

1 | Soak porcini mushrooms in lukewarm water for about 30 minutes.

2 | In the meantime, peel potatoes and grate finely. Clean white or cremini mushrooms and dice finely. Rinse green onions, clean, and chop finely. Rinse chervil, shake dry, and chop finely.

Drain porcini mushrooms and chop finely.

3 | Combine potatoes, mushrooms, onions, chervil, egg, and flour. Season with salt and pepper and stir well.

4 | In a large pan, heat butter and oil. Using a tablespoon, place small mounds of the potato mixture in the pan and fry over medium heat for 3–4 minutes on each side.

➤ Side dishes: Cucumber yogurt and salad or spinach leaves

Inexpensive | Fast
Mushroom with Potatoes and Onions

SERVES 4:

➤ ¾ lb cremini, oyster, or
  porcini mushrooms
  1 ⅔ lb unpeeled,
  cooked potatoes
  ¼ lb cooked ham
  2 large onions
  2 tbs clarified butter
  2 tsp caraway seeds
  ½ bunch fresh parsley

3 eggs
3 tbs milk
Salt
Freshly ground pepper

🕐 Prep time: 25 minutes
➤ Calories/serving: About 305

1 | Clean mushrooms and cut into slices or strips ⅛ inch thick. Peel potatoes and cut into ⅛ inch slices. Cut larger slices in half. Cut ham into thin strips. Peel onions, cut in half, and cut into strips.

2 | In a pan, heat clarified butter and sauté onions and ham over medium heat for 2–3 minutes. Add mushrooms and sauté for 2 minutes. Stir in potatoes and caraway and sauté for 5 minutes, stirring frequently.

3 | In the meantime, rinse parsley, shake dry, and chop leaves finely. Mix parsley with eggs and milk and season with salt and pepper. Also season the potato mixture to taste. Pour eggs over the top, mix well, and cook only until it sets.

Classic with a New Twist | Can Prepare in Advance

Gnocchi with Mushroom Cream Sauce

SERVE 4:

- ➤ 2 1/4 lb floury potatoes
  Salt
  3 tbs dried
  porcini mushrooms
  2/3 cup flour
  1/2 cup durum wheat
  semolina
  1 1/3 lb porcini, king oyster,
  or cremini mushrooms
  2 tbs lemon juice
  2 tbs butter
  2/3 cup vegetable stock
  1 cup heavy cream
  Freshly ground pepper
  1 tbs chopped
  fresh parsley

- ⏱ Prep time: 1 hour
- ⏱ Marinating time: 1 hour to
  1 day
- ➤ Calories/serving: About 595

1 | Cook potatoes in salted water for about 20 minutes until tender. Pour water off potatoes and let cool a little, but peel while still hot. Press through a potato ricer.

2 | Chop dried mushrooms in a food processor. Knead together potatoes, flour, semolina, and salt to form a dough.

3 | Form dough into long rolls the thickness of an index finger. Cut into pieces 1 inch long and flatten slightly with a fork. Let stand for at least 1 hour (preferably for 1 day).

4 | Clean fresh mushrooms, slice thinly, and mix with lemon juice. Simmer gnocchi in salted water for 10 minutes. Sauté mushrooms in butter for 3–4 minutes while stirring. Pour in stock and cream and reduce until thick and creamy. Season with salt and pepper.

5 | Mix parsley into mushrooms. Using a slotted spoon, remove gnocchi from water and arrange on mushrooms.

TIP | BAVARIAN PRETZEL DUMPLINGS

Slice 14 stale soft pretzels and soak in 1 1/2 cups lukewarm milk for 20 minutes. Knead together with 3 eggs, 1 chopped onion, 2 tablespoons chopped parsley, salt, and pepper. Shape into 8 dumplings and cook like gnocchi for 15 minutes.

> 1 **Knead dough**
Knead ingredients well until dough is workable and doesn't stick to your fingers.

> 2 **Shape gnocchi**
Carefully press dough pieces with the tines of a fork in order to make a pattern.

> 3 **Cook gnocchi**
Place gnocchi in boiling salted water. Reduce heat and simmer.

Fruity | Impressive

Mushrooms in Orange Sauce

SERVE 4:

- 1 1/3 lb mixed mushrooms (e.g. cremini, shiitake, and oyster mushrooms)

  1 1/3 cups small shallots

  Salt

  1/2 bunch thyme

  1 red chile pepper

  4 tbs olive oil

  4 juice oranges (preferably blood oranges)

  1/2 cup heavy cream

  3 tsp small capers

  1 pinch sugar

- ⏱ Prep time: 30 minutes
- ➤ Calories/serving: About 255

1 | Clean mushrooms and cut into thin slices or strips. Peel shallots and precook in salted water for 5 minutes. Plunge into cold water and drain.

2 | Rinse thyme, shake dry, and strip leaves from stems. Rinse chile pepper, remove stem and seeds, and cut into fine rings.

3 | Heat oil and sauté shallots with chile pepper and thyme over medium heat for 2–3 minutes. Add mushrooms and sauté for about 4 minutes.

4 | Squeeze juice from oranges. Add juice and cream to mushrooms. Season with capers and sugar and reduce until thick and creamy. Season with salt.

- ➤ Side dish: Rosemary potatoes
- ➤ Beverage: Light red wine

Fast | Inexpensive

Stir-Fried Mushrooms and Celery

SERVES 4:

- 4 stalks celery

  4 cloves garlic

  1 piece fresh ginger (about 2 inch)

  1 1/3 lb shiitake, cremini, or oyster mushrooms

  1 cup cherry tomatoes

  1 bunch fresh basil

  3 tbs oil

  1 tbs curry powder

  3/4 cup vegetable stock

  Salt

  2 green onions

- ⏱ Prep time: 20 minutes
- ➤ Calories/serving: About 160

1 | Rinse celery, clean, and slice thinly. Peel garlic and ginger and dice finely.

2 | Clean mushrooms. Remove stems from shiitake or oyster mushrooms and cut into strips. Cut cremini mushrooms into quarters. Rinse tomatoes and cut in half. Strip basil leaves from stems.

3 | Heat a wok or large pan and add oil. Stir-fry celery, mushrooms, ginger, and garlic for 3–4 minutes. Dust with curry powder and brown. Add vegetable stock, stir in tomatoes, season with salt, and bring to a boil over high heat.

4 | Rinse green onions, clean, cut into fine rings, and sprinkle over mushroom-vegetable mixture.

- ➤ Side dish: Aromatic or basmati rice
- ➤ Beverage: Beer

Can Prepare in Advance
Multicolored Mushrooms au Gratin

SERVE 4:
- ➤ 1 lb cremini, chanterelle, or oyster mushrooms
- 1 large red bell pepper
- 4 stalks celery
- 1 medium zucchini
- 2 cloves garlic
- 1 red onion
- 2 tomatoes
- 4 tbs olive oil
- 1 tbs capers (may substitute olives)
- Salt
- Freshly ground pepper
- 2 mozzarella balls (¼ lb each)

🕐 Prep time: 35 minutes
➤ Calories/serving: About 310

1 | Preheat oven to 450°F. Clean mushrooms and cut into quarters or strips. Rinse bell pepper, clean, and dice finely. Rinse celery and zucchini, clean, and slice thinly. Peel garlic and onion and chop finely. Rinse tomatoes, remove cores, and dice.

2 | In a pan, heat oil and sauté mushrooms for 2 minutes while stirring. Add bell pepper, celery, zucchini, garlic, and onion and sauté over medium heat for 3 minutes.

3 | Stir tomatoes and capers into mushroom mixture and season with salt and pepper. Transfer to a baking dish. Slice mozzarella finely and distribute on top. Bake in the oven (middle rack) for about 15 minutes until the cheese is melted and slightly brown.

➤ Side dish: Potatoes boiled in their skins
➤ Beverage: Red wine

For Company | Easy
Mushroom Quiche

SERVES 4:
- ➤ ½ cup cold butter
- 1 cup flour
- Salt
- Freshly ground pepper
- 2 tsp dried porcini mushrooms
- 1⅓ lb white mushrooms
- 2 tbs lemon juice
- 1 bunch green onions
- 1 bunch fresh parsley
- 4 eggs
- ½ cup freshly grated hard cheese
- 1 cup heavy cream

🕐 Prep time: 1¾ hours
➤ Calories/serving: About 755

1 | Dice butter and knead together with flour, salt, pepper, and 6 tablespoons water to form a smooth dough. Roll out dough, line a springform pan (11–12 inch diameter) with the dough, and refrigerate for 1 hour.

2 | Soak porcini mushrooms in lukewarm water. Clean white mushrooms, cut into thick slices, and toss with lemon juice. Rinse green onions, clean, and cut into fine rings. Rinse parsley, shake dry, and chop leaves finely. Preheat oven to 375°F.

3 | Drain porcini mushrooms and chop finely. Combine white mushrooms, onion rings and parsley, season with salt and pepper, and arrange on top of the dough. Thoroughly whisk together eggs, cheese, and cream and pour on top. Bake in the oven (middle rack) for about 45 minutes.

Mushrooms with Fish and Meat

Whether stir-fried in a pan, baked in the oven, or stewed in a pot, mushrooms taste heavenly with fish, meat, and poultry. Some can be ready in a flash, while others can be prepared in advance—which also makes them the ideal, stress-free choice for entertaining favorite guests. Try mushrooms and meat stir-fried in a wok, with oven-baked fish, or juicy chicken and mushrooms in a Dutch oven.

Quick Recipes

Asian Beef and Mushrooms

SERVES 4:

➤ ⅔ lb shiitake mushrooms | 1⅓ lb
fillet of beef | 2 stalks lemon grass |
4 cloves garlic | 2 chile peppers | 4 tbs
oil | ¾ cup Asian stock (store-bought) |
2 tbs soy sauce | 1 tbs lime juice | Salt

1 | Clean mushrooms and cut beef into
thin strips. Rinse lemon grass and cut
into pieces ¾ inch long. Peel garlic and
slice. Rinse chile peppers, clean, and cut
into rings.

2 | Sauté beef in oil for 2 minutes, remove
from the pan, and sauté mushrooms,
lemon grass, garlic, and chiles for 2 minutes. Stir in beef. Add stock and season to
taste with soy sauce, lime juice, and salt.
Serve with rice.

Mushroom Saltimbocca

SERVES 4:

➤ 1 lb large mushrooms (e.g. portobello,
porcini, oyster mushrooms) | ⅓ lb
raw ham, thinly sliced | 6 sprigs fresh
sage | Salt | Freshly ground pepper |
4 tbs butter | 6 tbs white wine

1 | Clean mushrooms and cut each
portobello or porcini mushroom in half
either crosswise or lengthwise. Cut ham
to the size of the mushrooms. Rinse sage,
shake dry, and pull off leaves.

2 | Season mushrooms with salt and pepper.
Top each mushroom with 1 slice ham and
2–3 sage leaves. Secure with toothpicks.
Sauté mushrooms in butter over medium
heat for 2–3 minutes on each side. Add
wine. Serve with white bread.

47

Can Prepare in Advance
Fish Fillets with Mushroom Cheese Topping

SERVES 4:

➤ ¾ lb cremini, white, or porcini mushrooms

4 fish fillets (about 6 oz each; e.g. white halibut or Victoria bass)

2 tbs lemon juice

2 tomatoes

2 cloves garlic

1 bunch basil

⅓ cup freshly grated Parmesan

4 tbs olive oil

Salt

Freshly ground pepper

🕙 Prep time: 35 minutes

➤ Calories/serving: About 360

1 | Preheat oven to 450°F. Clean mushrooms, cut half into slices almost ⅛ inch thick, and distribute in a baking dish. Rinse fish fillets under cold water, pat dry, and drizzle lemon juice.

2 | Chop remaining mushrooms very finely. Rinse tomatoes, remove cores, and dice finely. Peel garlic and chop finely. Pluck off basil leaves and chop finely.

3 | Knead together chopped mushrooms, tomatoes, garlic, basil, cheese, oil, salt, and pepper.

4 | Season fish fillets with salt and pepper and place in the baking dish. Spread mushroom mixture over the fish and press down lightly. Bake in the oven (middle rack) for about 15 minutes.

➤ Side dishes: Potatoes and arugula salad

➤ Beverage: White wine

Easy
Foil-Wrapped Fish

SERVES 4:

➤ 1½ lb fish fillet (e.g. halibut or redfish)

3 tbs lemon juice

⅔ lb cremini, oyster, or porcini mushrooms

3 tbs butter

1 bunch mixed fresh herbs

Salt

Freshly ground pepper

2 tbs crème fraîche

🕙 Prep time: 40 minutes

➤ Calories/serving: About 275

1 | Rinse fish fillet under cold water, pat dry, and drizzle with lemon juice. Clean mushrooms and cut into thin slices or strips. Sauté in 2 tablespoons butter over medium heat for 2–3 minutes.

2 | Preheat oven to 450°F. Rinse herbs, shake dry, and chop leaves finely. Mix with mushrooms and season with salt and pepper.

3 | Distribute half the mushrooms on a large sheet of aluminum foil. Season fish fillet with salt and pepper and place on top. Cover with remaining mushrooms and remaining butter cut into bits. Close foil and bake fish in the oven (middle rack) for 20 minutes.

4 | Open foil and transfer fish to preheated plates. Mix mushrooms with crème fraîche and heat briefly. Distribute over the fish.

Impressive
Fish with Tomato Mushrooms

SERVES 4:

➤ ⅗ lb tomatoes

2 medium zucchini

1 bunch green onions

4 cloves garlic

½ bunch fresh thyme

¾ lb cremini or white mushrooms

4 tbs olive oil

Salt

Freshly ground pepper

1 bunch fresh parsley

4 whole, cleaned fish (about ½ lb each; e.g. red mullet, sea bass, char)

🕐 Prep time: 1 hour

➤ Calories/serving: About 285

1 | Remove cores from tomatoes, blanch, peel, and dice. Rinse zucchini, clean, cut in half lengthwise, and slice crosswise.

2 | Preheat oven to 375°F. Rinse green onions, clean, and cut into fine rings. Peel garlic and slice finely. Rinse thyme, shake dry, and strip off leaves. Clean mushrooms

and cut in half or quarters, depending on their size.

3 | Mix tomatoes, zucchini, onion rings, garlic, thyme, mushrooms, and 3 table-spoons oil in a baking dish and season with salt and pepper. Bake in the oven (middle rack) for 10 minutes.

4 | Rinse parsley and shake dry. Rinse fish, season with salt and pepper inside and out, and fill with parsley. Arrange fish on top of vegetables, drizzle with oil, and bake for 30 minutes.

➤ Side dishes: Lemon wedges and rosemary potatoes

➤ Beverage: White wine

Asian | Easy
Mushrooms with Ginger and Shrimp

SERVES 4:

➤ 1 lb peeled shrimp

1 tbs soy sauce

1 tbs lemon juice

⅔ lb oyster or shiitake mushrooms

2 tomatoes

1 piece fresh ginger (about 1 inch)

3 tbs oil

2 tbs fish sauce

1 tsp sugar

Salt

Several fresh cilantro leaves

🕐 Prep time: 25 minutes

➤ Calories/serving: About 220

1 | Toss shrimp with soy sauce and lemon juice. Clean mushrooms, remove stems, and cut into strips. Rinse tomatoes and cut into eighths. Peel ginger and chop finely.

2 | Brown ginger briefly in oil. Add mushrooms and sauté for 2 minutes. Add shrimp and tomatoes and sauté over medium heat for 1 minute. Season to taste with fish sauce, sugar, and salt. Serve sprinkled with cilantro.

TIP

Instead of shrimp, you can also use firm fish fillet. Good with chile peppers.

Can Prepare in Advance
Sherry Chicken and Mushrooms

SERVES 4:

➤ 1 plump chicken (about 3½ lb)
Salt
Freshly ground pepper
4 cloves garlic
½ bunch fresh thyme
4 tbs olive oil
2 tbs black olives
1¼ cups dry sherry
2 bunches green onions
1⅓ cups sliced celery
¾ lb small white, cremini or chanterelle mushrooms
1 tbs butter

🕑 Prep time: 1¼ hours
➤ Calories/serving: About 615

1 │ Rinse chicken under cold water, pat dry, cut into 12 pieces, and season with salt and pepper. Peel garlic. Rinse thyme and shake dry.

2 │ In a Dutch oven, brown chicken thoroughly in half the oil over high heat and then remove. Add garlic, thyme, olives, and sherry to the Dutch oven.

3 │ Place chicken pieces (except for breast meat) in the sauce, cover, and stew over low heat for 25 minutes.

4 │ Rinse onions and celery, clean, and cut into pieces ¾ inch long. Clean mushrooms. Sauté mushrooms in remaining oil and butter for 2–3 minutes. Add remaining vegetables and sauté over medium heat for 3 minutes. Place breast meat in the Dutch oven and cook for another 25 minutes.

For Company │ Easy
Meat Rolls with Balsamic Vinegar

SERVES 4:

➤ 2 tsp dried porcini mushrooms
2 green onions
2 cloves garlic
1 bunch fresh parsley
1 mozzarella ball (about ¼ lb)
Salt
Freshly ground pepper
8 veal cutlets (about 3 oz each; may substitute turkey cutlets)
⅔ lb porcini or oyster mushrooms
1 beefsteak tomato
3 tbs oil
2 tbs balsamic vinegar

🕑 Prep time: 50 minutes
➤ Calories/serving: About 330

1 │ Soak dried mushrooms in ⅔ cup lukewarm water for 30 minutes. Then drain (save soaking water) and chop finely.

2 │ Rinse and clean onions, rinse parsley and shake dry, and chop both finely. Dice mozzarella, mix with chopped porcini mushrooms, onions, garlic and half the parsley, and season with salt and pepper.

3 │ Press cutlets flat, spread mixture on top, and roll up. Secure the ends with toothpicks and season meat rolls with salt and pepper.

4 │ Clean fresh mushrooms and slice finely. Pour boiling water over tomatoes, peel, and dice. Brown meat rolls thoroughly in oil. Add mushrooms and sauté briefly. Add soaking water and tomatoes, cover, and stew over low heat for 10 minutes. Season with vinegar, salt and pepper, and sprinkle with parsley.

Middle-Eastern | Inexpensive

Lamb and Mushroom Stew

SERVES 4:

➤ ¾ lb cremini mushrooms (as small as possible)

⅔ lb carrots

1 lb deboned lamb (leg or lean shoulder)

1 onion

2 cloves garlic

4 tbs olive oil

Salt

Freshly ground pepper

1 tsp each of hot Hungarian paprika, cumin, and coriander

¼ tsp cinnamon

1 small jar saffron (ground or threads, 0.1 g)

🕐 Prep time: 1¼ hours
➤ Calories/serving: About 270

1 | Clean mushrooms and, if necessary, cut larger ones in half. Peel carrots and cut into pieces ¾ inch long. Cut lamb into ¾ inch cubes. Peel onion and garlic and chop.

2 | In a Dutch oven, heat half the oil and sear lamb over high heat in 2 batches,

removing each batch when done. Sauté mushrooms and carrots in remaining oil for about 2 minutes. Stir in onion and garlic, add 1¼ cups water, and loosen pan residues. Add lamb.

3 | Season lamb and vegetables to taste with salt, pepper, and all the seasonings (stir saffron into a little water and then add). Cover and stew over low heat for about 45 minutes until tender.

➤ Side dish: Couscous
➤ Beverage: Red wine

For Company | Classic

Veal Ragout with Morels

SERVES 4:

➤ ⅛ cup dried morels

1 cup small shallots

2 young kohlrabi

2 tbs oil

1 tbs butter

1½ lb veal stew meat, cut into large cubes

½ cup dry white wine (may substitute veal stock)

Salt

Freshly ground pepper

2 tbs chopped fresh chervil

½ cup crème fraîche

1 tbs lemon juice

🕐 Prep time: 45 minutes
🕐 Soaking time: 1 hour
➤ Calories/serving: About 435

1 | Soak morels in ¾ cup lukewarm water for 1 hour, then rinse well, and cut in half. Filter soaking water. Peel shallots and kohlrabi and cut kohlrabi into thick sticks.

2 | Heat butter in a Dutch oven, sear veal in batches, and then remove. Brown shallots and morels in pan drippings and add wine and morel soaking water. Add veal, season with salt and pepper, and stew over low heat for 30 minutes. After 10 minutes, stir in kohlrabi.

3 | Stir chervil and crème fraîche into stew. Season to taste with salt, pepper, and lemon juice.

➤ Side dish: Rice
➤ Beverage: White wine

Photo top: **Veal Ragout with Morels**   *Photo bottom:* **Lamb and Mushroom Stew** ➤

Inexpensive | Hearty
Meatball Gratin

SERVES 4:

- ➤ 1 stale roll
  - ½ cup milk
  - 1 ½ lb floury potatoes
  - ¾ lb cremini mushrooms
  - Salt
  - Freshly ground pepper
  - 2 tbs olive oil
  - 1 cup meat stock
  - 4 cloves garlic
  - ½ bunch fresh thyme
  - 1 lb mixed ground meat
  - 1 egg
  - 1 tsp Hungarian sweet paprika

- ⏱ Prep time: 30 minutes
- ⏱ Baking time: 40 minutes
- ➤ Calories/serving: About 565

1 | Soak roll in milk. Peel potatoes and slice. Clean mushrooms and slice.

2 | Preheat oven to 375°F. Layer potatoes and mushrooms in a shallow baking dish, seasoning each layer with salt and pepper, and drizzling with oil. Pour in stock around the edges.

3 | Peel garlic and mince. Rinse thyme, shake dry, and strip off leaves. Squeeze out roll and shred. Thoroughly knead together roll, garlic, thyme, ground meat, and egg. Season to taste with salt, pepper, and paprika.

4 | Shape meat mixture into small balls and place on top of the gratin. Bake in the oven (middle rack) for about 40 minutes until potatoes are tender.

- ➤ Side dish: Tossed salad
- ➤ Beverage: Red wine

For Gourmets | Classic
Swiss-Style Veal with Asparagus

SERVES 4:

- ➤ 1 lb veal fillet (may substitute pork fillet)
  - ½ lb cremini or king oyster mushrooms
  - ½ lb green asparagus
  - 1 bunch green onions
  - 1 tbs oil
  - 1 tbs butter
  - 1 tbs flour
  - ¾ cup meat stock
  - ½ cup heavy cream
  - Salt
  - Freshly ground pepper
  - 2 tsp lemon juice

- ⏱ Prep time: 30 minutes
- ➤ Calories/serving: About 370

1 | Cut meat into thin strips. Clean mushrooms and slice finely. Rinse asparagus, trim ends generously, and cut into ¾ inch pieces. Rinse green onions, trim, and cut into fine rings.

2 | Heat oil and butter and sear meat over high heat in 2 batches, removing each batch when done. Thoroughly brown mushrooms, asparagus, and onion rings in the fat.

3 | Dust with flour, add stock, cover, and stew over low heat for 5 minutes. Stir in cream and reduce sauce slightly. Stir in meat and season to taste with salt, pepper, and lemon juice.

- ➤ Side dish: Fried potatoes or ribbon pasta
- ➤ Beverage: White wine

Glossary

Balsamic vinegar
Vinegar that wears a controlled origin designation (DOC) comes from the Modena and Emilia-Romagna provinces and is mainly produced from white Trebbiano grapes. The older the vinegar, the more intensely seasoned and the milder its flavor. A white variety is also available, called white balsamic vinegar. This type is very mild, but is not produced according to the traditional process.

Chile peppers
Whether these little peppers are fresh or dried, most of their heat resides in their white seeds. So if you want to spice your dish more conservatively, be sure to remove them (for fresh chile peppers, also remove the white interior membrane to which the seeds are attached) or at least use only part of them. Important: Wash your hands thoroughly and do not rub your eyes, because the fiery oils adhere to your skin.

Fish sauce
Fish and shrimp are mixed with salt and allowed to ferment. Fish sauce is the extract from this tangy mixture. It almost smells a little musty and is intensely flavorful. Together with lime juice, it gives many Asian dishes their kick.

Stocks, store-bought
Whether they have a vegetable, fish, game, poultry, beef, or even mushroom base, store-bought stocks never taste as good as homemade, but are still better than using bouillon cubes. They're so concentrated that you can dilute them with water.

Fontina
This fine melting cheese from the Valle d'Aosta is made from cow's milk and very frequently used for cooking in Italy. It ripens for about 5 months in caves, which is how it gets its wonderfully aromatic flavor.

Ginger
Freshly chopped or grated, ginger adds bite and lots of flavor. The fresh root is peeled like a potato and then chopped.

Capers
These spicy buds from the caper bush are harvested before they blossom and are available in two forms: Pickled in a vinegar liquid or preserved in salt. Pickled capers are available in any supermarket. The salty variety can be found in Italian delicatessens. The latter are much spicier and must be rinsed thoroughly to remove the salt.

Mozzarella
This fine fresh cheese was originally produced from buffalo milk, although most of today's mozzarella is made from cow's milk. If you want to eat mozzarella plain, try the buffalo milk variety (mozzarella di bufala). It's softer and is much more flavorful.

Olive oil

Tangy in taste, olive oil goes especially well with mushrooms. For cooked dishes, you should use cold-pressed olive oil. But save the finest oil from the noblest olives for salads and other cold dishes. This is where its flavor is best revealed.

Pine nuts

These fine, aromatic, and sweet tasting seeds must be removed from pinecones using a complex process, which explains why they're so expensive. They taste even better if you toast them in an ungreased pan until golden. Pine nuts have a fairly high fat content, so they won't keep for very long.

Polenta

Unlike coarse cornmeal, polenta is ground finely. In Italy, polenta is served as a side dish, but they also use it to make main dishes. Besides normal polenta that cooks in about 30 minutes, there is also instant polenta that takes only 5 minutes and is also delicious.

Risotto rice

This Italian medium-grain rice comes from the Po valley, which is also where the most risotto is eaten. When cooked, the rice grains become tender outside while their interiors remain slightly firm, like perfectly cooked al dente pasta. The best varieties are vialone and carnaroli, but arborio and avorio are also used.

Saffron

These fine threads (stigmas from a type of crocus) have long been one of the world's most expensive spices — which is why there tend to be imitations. Gently rub saffron threads between your fingers and stir into warm liquid before adding to a dish. You can also buy ground saffron, but it doesn't have nearly as powerful a flavor.

Shallots

The aroma of these fine French onions is both more intense and milder than typical cooking onions. Because they're so nice and small, you can easily cook them whole.

Mustard

Mustard is made from mustard powder (from various mustard seeds), vinegar, spices, and water. It ranges from mild to very hot, depending on which mustard seeds are used. One of the most flavorful is hot Dijon mustard, which comes from the city of Dijon in Burgundy.

Walnuts

Like mushrooms, walnuts are ready to harvest in the fall and the two go well together. It's best to buy them in the shell and crack them open yourself. Like all nuts, they keep longer in the shell.

Lemon grass

These thin stalks are available in any Asian market. Lemon grass gives foods a fine lemon-lime aroma. First remove the outer leaves, then flatten the stalk slightly, and cook them whole. You can also chop lemon grass very finely and serve it on the side.

Using this Index
To help you find recipes
containing certain ingredients
more quickly, this index also
lists favorite ingredients (such
as **balsamic vinegar** or **pasta**)
in **bold type**, followed by the
corresponding recipes.

The Author

Cornelia Schinharl is interested in anything related to food and drink. For over 15 years, she has been putting her wealth of experience down on paper as both a food journalist and a cookbook author. She never seems to run out of new ideas. For this project as well, she came up with a number of new creations that will make your mouth water.

The Photographer

After completing his studies at a photography school in Berlin, **Michael Brauner** worked as an assistant to renowned photographers in France and Germany before striking out on his own in 1984. His unique, atmospheric style is valued highly everywhere, as much in advertising firms as by noted European publishers.

Photo Credits

Cover photo: Jörn Rynio, Hamburg
All others: Michael Brauner

Published originally under the title Pilze: Rezepte rund ums Jahr © 2003 Gräfe und Unzer Verlag GmbH, Munich. English translation for the U.S. market © 2006 Silverback Books, Inc.

Program director: Doris Birk
Managing editor: Birgit Rademacker
Translator: Christie Tam (US)
Editor: Stefanie Poziombka, Lisa M. Tooker (US)
Proofreading, typesetting, DTP: Redaktionsbüro Christina Kempe, Munich
Layout, typography and cover design: Independent Medien Design, Munich
Production: Helmut Giersburg, Patty Holden (US)

ISBN 1-59637-061-0

Enjoy Other Quick & Easy Books

Cooking for One

Christina Kempe

Cocktails & Mixed Drinks

Tanja Dusy & Alessandra Redies

Bread Machine

Elise A. Hanes

Cooking for Children

V. Cramm

Preserves and Canning

Irresistible Fondue

Angelika Illies

Cooking for Two

Cornelia Adam

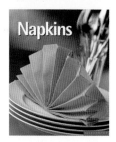

Napkins

Fast Italian

Margit Proebst

Sushi

Andreas Furtmayr

Clever ideas from Japan
and new fusion sushi
Home-made perfectly

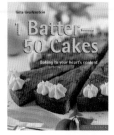

1 Batter— 50 Cakes

Nina Greifenstein

Baking to your heart's content

Cooking in Clay

Healthy Recipes with Great Flavor

Erika Casparek-Türkkan

Coffee and Espresso

Tanja Dusy

Grilling

Antje Gruener

Sauces and Dips

Soups

Classic to Contemporary

Sebastian Dickhaut

Raclette

Claudia Schmidt

New Recipes with Cheese Primer and Party Dips

Antipasti and Tapas

Mediterranean Appetizers

Cornelia Schinharl

1 Pan— 50 Muffins

Salads

Cornelia Adam

An array of salads to eat as
appetizers, entrees, and party
dishes. Includes classic choices
and cutting-edge alternatives.

Sandwiches

Tanja Burgtorf

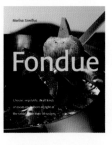

Fondue

Marlisa Szwillus

Cheese, vegetable, broth kinds
of meat–conjured all right at
the table. More than 50 recipes.

Christmas Cookies

PREPARING MUSHROOMS

- With a knife, scrape off only the spots that are really dirty.
- Otherwise, just wipe with a damp paper towel.
- If the skin is already fairly wrinkled, it's better to peal it off. However, a mushroom that looks like this is really no longer fresh enough.
- Always wait to cut up mushrooms until shortly before using.

Guaranteed Perfect Mushroom Recipes

SIGNS OF FRESHNESS

- Fresh mushrooms also smell fresh, not musty or even slightly fishy.
- Fresh mushrooms look plump and dry, but not dried out.
- Fresh mushrooms have no discolored or moldy spots.

THE RIGHT HERBS

- Mushrooms are very compatible with sour herbs, such as chervil, lemon balm, and sorrel.
- When sautéed or grilled, mushrooms go best with Mediterranean herbs, such as rosemary, thyme, and sage.
- In a salad, mushrooms taste best with arugula, watercress, or wild garlic.

GARNISH

- Dishes look nice when you slice up a few raw mushrooms and scatter them over the top before serving.
- Herbs and lemon peel are always appropriate.
- Toasted pine nuts look and taste great.